Musings from the Teenage Soul

I0201345

Myisha Velez
Nyangel Velez

Mutual Blessings Books
Huntsville, AL
MBSuccess@karenmaloy.org
www.karenmaloy.org

No part of this book may be reproduced or transmitted in any form or by any means electronically or mechanically, including photocopying and recording, or by any information storage or retrieval system, except as may be expressly permitted in writing by the publisher. Requests for permission should be addressed in writing to: MB Success Strategies at MBSuccess@karenmaloy.org. To order additional copies of this resource: write MB Success Strategies at MBSuccess@karenmaloy.org; call orders at (315) 657-3648 or order online at www.karenmaloy.org.

Printed in the United States of America

Musings of the Teenage Soul
Mutual Blessings Books
Publisher/Editor: MB Success Strategies
Published by Mutual Blessings Books - Huntsville, AL 35816
1-315-657-3648 - Website: **www.karenmaloy.org**

Printed in the United States of America. All rights reserved under International Copyright Law. Contents and/or cover may not be reproduced in whole or in part in any form without the express written consent of the publisher.

Copyright © 2013 Myisha & Nyangel Velez
All rights reserved.
ISBN-10: 0985660856
ISBN-13: 978-0985660857

DEDICATION

To my parents, David and Karen, for all of
their support. As well as my dear confidant
ShaCorry, you were my inspiration.
- Myisha

Thank you for my mom Karen and friend
Emmanuel for supporting and inspiring me.
- Nyangel

CONTENTS

MYISHA & NYANGEL VELEZ

ACKNOWLEDGMENTS

We would like to thank our mother for all of her help during this process. She gave us the support we needed to go through with it

FEAR

You may think you know
I do.
Don't become the one they fear
Don't become the fool.
Death is all around
Please don't kill
For you are found
People love you
You don't need to prove anything
God loves you too
Let's be friends
Don't use your fists
Some fear being alone
Go out with friends
Use the phone
Do things to stay away from fear
Talk to anyone
Somebody's always near

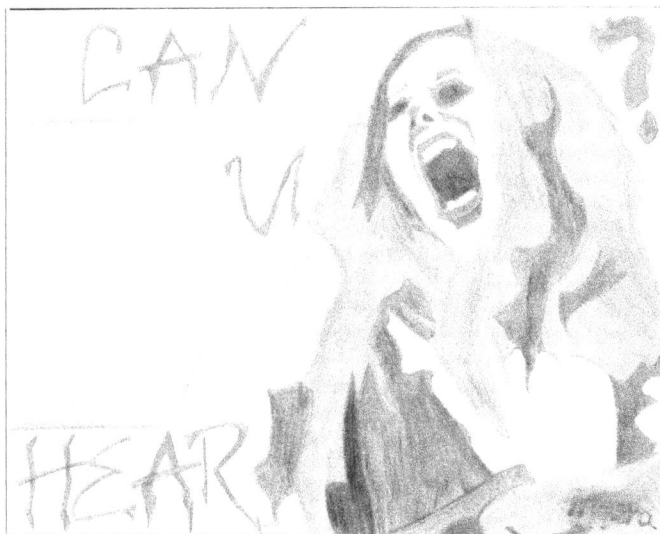

BIRTHDAYS

All those birthdays thinking he didn't want me
Then eight months before my next, I found
out he wasn't mine
I thought, how can this be?
I met the real one later that day
A few weeks late
Unknowingly taking the test
And three days later being told
And not knowing what to say
That new man is my father
Before then I never knew him
I wanted to call the old one.
 But why bother?
The next time he saw me
We had fun shopping together
A smile on my face is all that could be seen

Last weekend I stayed at his house
I met my brother, step- mother and slept in my
sister's room
Feeling as though I was invading their privacy;
an invasion not unlike a mouse
Now I'm used to them
And I have fun too
Forever that will be in my mind; as my
memories

TO YOU

Is there love or is there not
It might still be but you've forgot.
Out of everything that used to be
You have lost your sight;
For you no longer see
As these tears continue to fall from my eyes
Because you're not here
You've spread those wings to fly.
It seemed as the perfect fix
but in the end,
It simply didn't mix.
I won't give up
I'll continue to fight
Until you walk away from darkness
Into the light.
I'll be waiting
If you decide to come ask
Without each other
There's just something we lack
So remember that
Next time you look at her face
For being your girl
Used to be *my* rightful place

DONE WAITING

Done waiting
For something that'll never come
I'm surrounded by others
While still totally alone
Tears falling from my eye
For through everything that's happened
I was completely blind
She's there for you
In ways I'll never be
It's always been there
But now I see
You're making your bed
And I'm making mine
Everything has been said
We just need time
It's the cure
For this continuous addiction

The workers are ready
For this tenuous construction
Everything will stay the same
Nothing will change
No one here is clearly to blame
I'll try to do me
While you do you
Sooner than you think
It may emerge as something new

YOU TOOK SO LONG

You took so long
To tell me what I never thought I'd hear
That the feeling wouldn't be mutual
Was what was told you fear
Thoughts that come and go
As long as I've known you
Yes, they began and never lost their touch
Something I've become accustomed to
I've ignored it
For my loyalty to another
I wouldn't dare ruin these friendships
So why even bother?
This reminds me of another situation
In which I'd repeatedly gave you advice
Endless conversations
The funny thing is,
That you probably would've never told me
If we'd never chose to leave
Only when you wouldn't have to see me
Doesn't complicate things
Only now I know more
Our friendship will remain the same
As it was before

FEELINGS

Through the years
She's ignored the feelings
Of loneliness and constantly being taken
advantage of
 Consistently releasing tears after supposed
bouts of meetings
Being used by anyone possible
And thrown away when done.
Never with a day of peace
A day without sadness; with smiles and lots of
fun
Never to let anyone know
Of the fake smiles and blank eyes
The translucent wall invisible to all but her
Ever present bickering and fist fights
Being loud and telling jokes
Making her fun to be around
No one could tell how much she hurt
The need for silence to be filled with sound
Teenage years are hard
Hers feeling to be more than others
An incredible selfishness
A need to be away
A fear of without reason
No mission for being brought into this world.

An extending loneliness from the seat she's
upon
A recollection of someone saying
While in the throes of a story
A grain of truth fell in which teenagers were
committing suicide
Yet it never occurred to you?
That it may eventually become of she?
Guess it was never to be seen.
Probably never will realize
How unhappiness radiated form her core
In the countless, sleepless nights
A stifled need to tell another
Wanting that relationship
But fearing that issue of trust

Yet it is too late now
She no longer wants to be helped
For she that failed her the most
Was herself

WITHOUT RESPONSE

Ever felt without a purpose?
Living a life not felt to be worth it?
A feeling of inferiority by any person you
meet?
A fear of the risk to trust?
Knowledge of the opposite sex's need for
intimate pleasure?
A defeated spirit without reason to try
anymore?
I have…
And frankly am without want to hear that
incriminating voice again…

I KNEW IT, YET STILL CRIED

I knew it, yet still cried
I asked for truth and received only lies
I've wondered;
Begging for an understanding
The conversation grew intense
Your voice more frightening.
How did this happen?
It was genuine and rang of truth
Guess I was wrong…
Must have been confused…
'Cuz for some time,
I believed myself enough for you

CURSES

Cursed my name
Cursed the rest
Cursed my worth
The ultimate test.
But when passing a mirror
I realized one thing:
I am beautiful
And shall remain with any change.

SUNS HAVE RISEN

Suns have risen
Suns have set
Full of memories
That won't forget.
Hearts have broken
Smiles are born
Colorful emotions
Have come around
Friends are few
Thoughts of, less.
Trained rather to follow
Than lead the rest
Life is here
In the now
Greeting with joy
Rather with sorrows to drown.

EVERYTHING'S CHANGED

Everything changed
Everything she once knew
Too young to comprehend
The stages she went through unable to
understand the pain
Her heart heavy; her eyes sore
Displaying a false sense of security
With the smile she wore
It didn't stop..
It couldn't end
Losing an endless battle..
Innocence is what she had.
Running from home
Quickening her footsteps as her tears hit the
gravel
Blaming herself
Each day gets worse

Punishing herself for sins others gathered
Like a blooming orchid rose
What was once beautiful and soft
Now thorns grow
But every human knows
With time the storm will go
and the clouds will go…
then the matured beautiful girl's smile will
show.

Yusef Jones and Myisha Velez

A SOUL'S REVELATION

his eyes; brown and constant as the stars
their attention focused, that no blow could waver
nothing unnoticed; stretching near and far
crying out in pain that he'll always remember

a light steadily brightening, yet denies
banned to the dark to search in envy
a battle of the great for his soulful eyes
glazing over in shock, as they're knocked into a frenzy

struggling with memories long torn from sight
racing to the battlefront for dominance
plaguing his eyesight; forcing him far behind the disfigured
night
projecting an air of supreme prominence

revealing nothing, and giving everything
and forever silent in his sould deep teachings

A BRIGHT LIGHT IN THE DARK OF NIGHT

to my family, I've always been quite bright
and while acknowledged with a tone so sweet
i shall not be missed in the dark of night.

every summer i darken using all my might
watching it leave once again in the season of wheat
it can't fail! i've always been quite bright.

and when it seems as though i'd finally hidden from sight
my spirit falls as my captor's and my face meet
for i can't be missed in the dark of night.

playful banter alongside the emergence of light
a familt of value; the scale so neat
next to my family, i've always been quite bright.
unwillingly racing the change with the speed of light
my true desire an unnattainable feat
i won't be missed in the dark of night.
watching snow fall as my tone reaches a new height
laughter ringing. ignoring the chill in our feet
alongside my family, I'm still considered quite bright
and i can't be missed in the dark of night

DECISIONS

it broke her heart
threw her down to her knees
she looked to the sky
begging and pleading
"Lord please help me.
i can't do this along"
when he opened his embrace
gathering her into his arms
"I'm here my child;
I'll never leave your side.
now I'm waiting,
for you to decide".

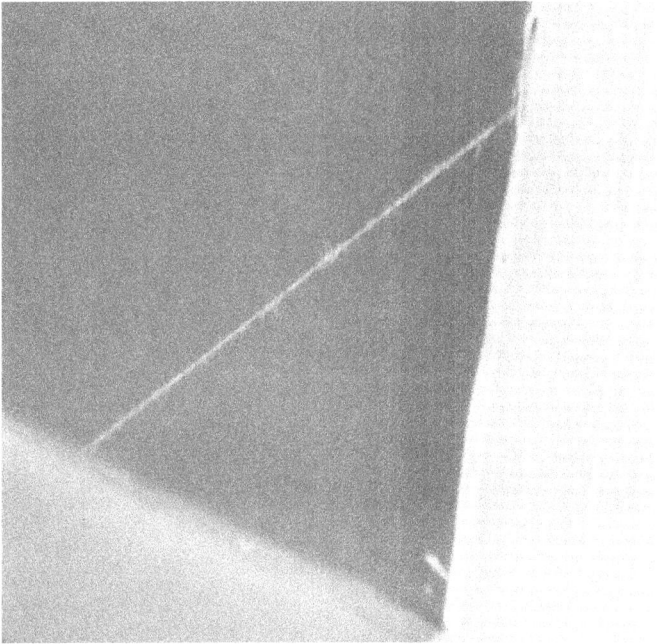

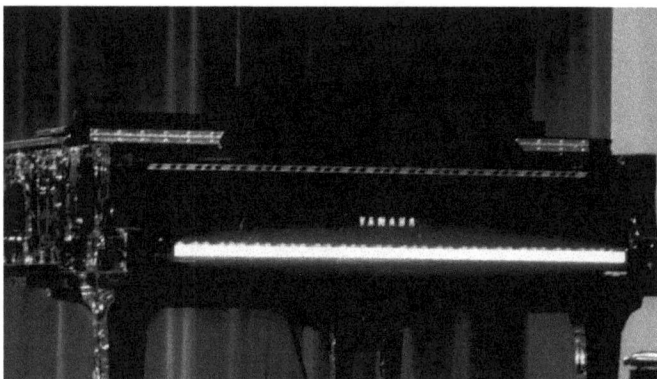

TO HIM I RETURN

to him i return
expressing as i yearn
for him
everything of him
a sweet Valentines' day to you i wish
throwing love across this distance-
sealed with a kiss

not for a day of hearts, and whistles,
and cheap bouquets
full of captivating clichés
but of our devotion holding forever and a day
dispelling whatever you may
that does not support that is to be
everything which is
you and me

INNER FEARS

a dark tunnel. seemingly,
never-ending and everlasting
the air damp; strangling the breath from my lungs
the walls cold against my fingertips
the floor chilling to my toes
my fear crippling; my steps uneven
not knowing
if the breath against my neck is real or just…
an extension of my being

the dead silence overtaken by a sudden choir of sound.
i burst into a run
escaping the noise; my thoughts… my terror
the steps behind me matching mine tenfold
my demons reaching out to take hold
evasion; elusion; abdication

stretching towards that
unperceived freedom
tunnel- vision inflexibly focused on my limitations
pushing, knowing, and fearing what is to be
leaping in a last act of desperation
and crumbling downwards as the
darkness overtakes my senses

"SINCE FEELINGS IS FIRST" BY E.E. CUMMINGS

"since feelings is first" by E.E. Cummings
without title; without justification.
lacking in clarification
mocking
who puts "any attention" into words who mean not;
who lacks the initiative to express as "wholly as actions
tend too.

a man. failing to know the sincerity
of the implication of feelings
"Wholly to be a fool"
before an epiphany makes real; how kisses are more
priceless than knowledge
detailed to provide images so true;
his desire changes to that of a manmade aware
the perception of she who is
susceptible to easy emotion more valuable than the
senseless thoughts of man
it cannot be insulted with few words on the
experiences of a lifetime
forbidden to summarize, or indeed merely
comprehend the extent to which actions communicate

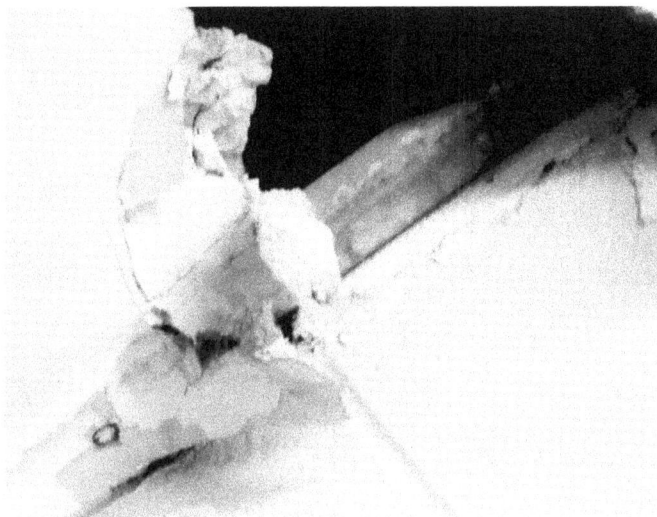

PROCLAMATIONS

i shall proclaim i miss you
yet we know it never ends…
hidden tears often make claims
the mouth is not yet ready to speak
limbs and their gestures gone unnoticed
a tightening in its hold, a blind reach for
something unseen;
a distant memory.
sleep a Bipolar, unforgiving and often
translucent friend
unreliable in moments of anguish
playing both sides of fear, as if
able to realize its implications
as if

able to feel the insecurities; the jealousy
and the pain
as if
my subconscious knows betrayal
a playing of the mind
revelations of secrets better left to their
hallucinatory devices
waiting for the moment when fear is born
into reality.
authentic to *my* reality.
praying you linger
as my reality
a celtic know impotent to all
treacherous falsehoods
wholly unsusceptible to bitches of greed,

covetness; a great eagerness for another's warranted
sentiments for what was yours,
transcendingly mine
to remain ours
relics impervious to falsified, opaque intentions

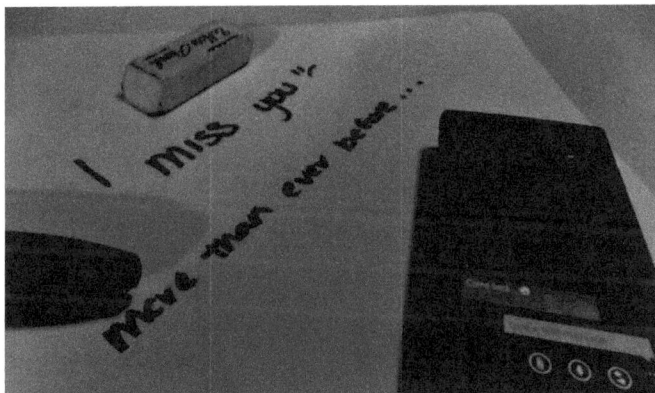

ONCE UPON A TIME…

lovely words
soft to the touch
melted.

fire from the lips
brushing my fingertips
racing down the wick as
thunderbolts.

hatred once the emergence of love
songs once swayed, yet never were understood
longing a fond, intense memory

pulsing with enough life; almost…
enough to breathe life into it once again

dull aches lulled falsely
cracks overturning the yearning
simple mistakes nevermore analyzed quite so simply.

words cutting deep…
far beyond where physical blows may reach…
longing.. longing.. longing

for what used to be

SOFT QUIPS MURMURED

soft quips of murmured unto the silence bound with
air
tearing a jagged line like fog through it's belly
a sun shines; ignoring its ivory legacy of beauty fair
protesting silent arrogance
floating its command: *"Tell me"*
secrets churning
unaware of danger cloaking the essence of life
ignoring troubles intent on mourning
preserving transparent happiness faked by a knife
men battling with swords; such evil provoking their
honor
women crying out against talons digging for the gold
hidden within
struggles met with shock and wonder
contrasting gruesome acts of times beyond a stitched
mend
purely existing to understand the colorful hues
tricked by the lure of wisdom;
yet none above the stench of fools

THE PAIN

The pain
Gripping for dear life on the strings of my
heart
Tears freefalling
Suicide missions leaping to their fate
Falling faster and faster
Easily mistaken for rain
Running gracefully in the slopes of my contour
lines

In reaction to fateful transmission calls
Unlikely to be ignored

"We'll always be friends My"
Told me it'll never end
A broken promise that fell from your lips
What happened to my friend?
Was he hurt, delivered great sorrow or simply..
never existed?
A relationship with another an extension of my
desperation..
Yet the figment seemingly so true?

A pain… the pain..
O, shall it never leave?
Please, oh please..

Please accept me.
My friend… my dear friend..
Where have you gone?

WHY CAN'T ANYONE HEAR ME?

I wake up every morning not knowing how I
feel
not knowing what I want
I give you all the signs, but I can see you that
you just don't get it
Why can't anyone hear me on the outside.
I show I don't care but on the insider I'm
screaming louder than you can imagine
Why can't anyone hear me?

When people tell me things I can't ever
imagine me believing them
The things you say and do to me you don't
know that it hurts me.
I don't know much about myself so, I just
make myself like whatever anyone else likes
Why can't you hear me?

I try so hard to be someone that I am not but,
I learned that God made us all different AND
that he loves me for me
Why can't anyone hear me?

You say that you love me and I try so hard to
believe you
But you can't make me feel important

And then you leave
You leave me with memories that I can't erase
I wonder if anyone could ever love me
If anyone but God can ever love me?

You call me names, I say that I don't care
But at the end of the day, I'm trying to change
myself.
People ask me what's wrong but I just say
nothing.
I want a friend that won't tell anyone what I
tell them
That won't feel bad for me
Someone who would help me and love me
I wonder, will my kids feel the same way I do?
I pray and I pray that God will help me but,
I don't have the strength to believe he will.
Why can't anyone hear me!!!!!!!!!

"LET ME OUT!" by Myisha Velez

TEARS AND FEARS

We as people are all alike in some way
We all shed tears and we all fear something in
our lifetime
But what we do with our tears and fears is
what makes us different from one another

UNANSWERED QUESTIONS

Unanswered questions all over the world
Unanswered questions all in my mind
I have a lot of unanswered questions
wondering who can answer at least of the them
besides God.
I have a lot of questions going through my
mind but I never ask them out loud

WHAT GOD SAID (ANSWERS)

You don't like yourself so much - do you?
You don't care what happens to you - do you?
You think that everything that happens to you
that you deserve it
Good or bad but mainly bad
You hate yourself more than anything or
anyone
Since you don't love yourself you think
everyone is lying to you but not all of them
Everything will be better if you will forgive
yourself

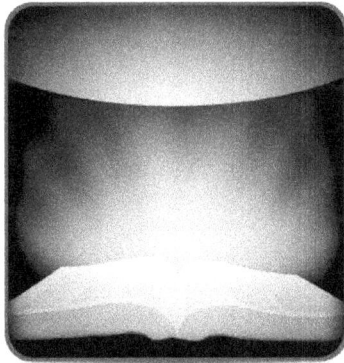

Musings From the Teenage Soul

by

Myisha Velez

&

Nyangel Velez

www.ingramcontent.com/pod-product-compliance
Lightning Source LLC
Chambersburg PA
CBHW071739020426
42331CB00008B/2096